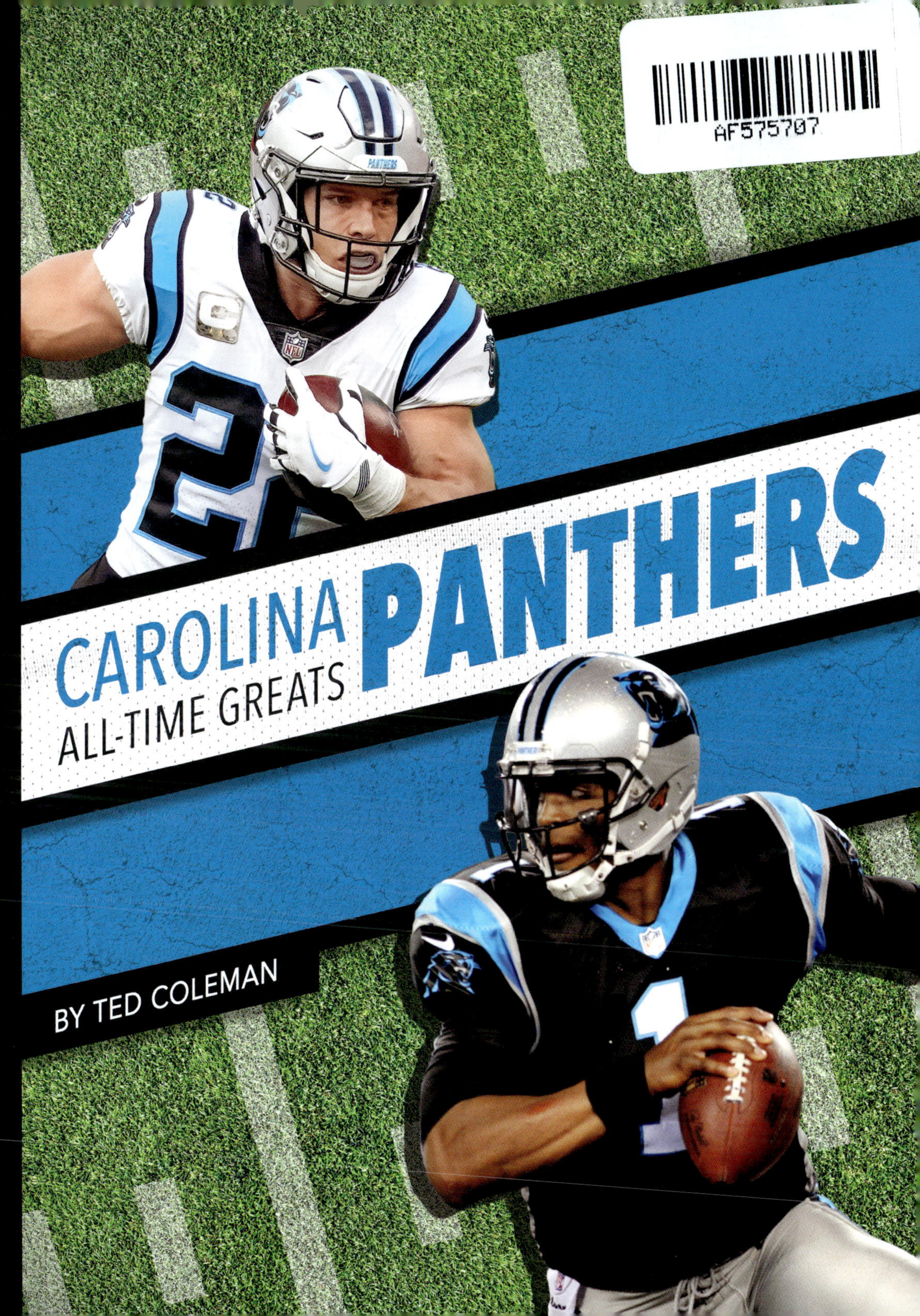
AF575707
CAROLINA
PANTHERS
ALL-TIME GREATS
BY TED COLEMAN

Book design by Jake Slavik
Cover design by Jake Slavik

Photographs ©: Jeff Roberson/AP Images, cover (top), 1 (top); Bill Kostroun/AP Images, cover (bottom), 1 (bottom); Al Bello/Getty Images Sport/Getty Images, 4; Craig Jones/Getty Images Sport/Getty Images, 7; Nick Laham/Getty Images Sport/Getty Images, 8; Streeter Lecka/Getty Images Sport/Getty Images, 9, 13; Dannie Walls/Icon Sportswire/Getty Images, 10; Scott Cunningham/Getty Images Sport/Getty Images, 15; Grant Halverson/Getty Images Sport/Getty Images, 16; Maddie Meyer/Getty Images Sport/Getty Images, 19; Jacob Kupferman/Getty Images Sport/Getty Images, 21

Press Box Books, an imprint of Press Room Editions.

ISBN
978-1-63494-422-9 (library bound)
978-1-63494-439-7 (paperback)
978-1-63494-472-4 (epub)
978-1-63494-456-4 (hosted ebook)

Library of Congress Control Number: 2021916615

Distributed by North Star Editions, Inc.
2297 Waters Drive
Mendota Heights, MN 55120
www.northstareditions.com

Printed in the United States of America
012022

ABOUT THE AUTHOR

Ted Coleman is a sportswriter who lives in Louisville, Kentucky, with his trusty Affenpinscher, Chloe.

TABLE OF CONTENTS

MILLS
51

CHAPTER 1
THE FIRST PANTHERS

The Carolina Panthers were a brand-new team in 1995. But that didn't mean all their players were new. Linebacker **Sam Mills** had spent nine years with the New Orleans Saints. As a Panther, Mills provided the team with leadership. He also showed that he still had plenty more to give. In 1996, Mills made the Pro Bowl. Best of all, he led the Panthers to the conference championship game.

Mills was not the only veteran on defense. Linebacker **Kevin Greene** was near the end of a Hall of Fame career. In 1996, the punishing pass rusher racked up 14.5 sacks. That was the most in the National Football League (NFL).

The 1996 Panthers didn't just rely on defense. **John Kasay** was a steady presence in the kicking game. Kasay spent 15 seasons with Carolina. During that time, he scored 1,482 points. Kasay remains the Panthers' all-time leading scorer.

Carolina had some excellent offensive weapons as well. Veteran tight end **Wesley Walls** joined the Panthers in 1996. Walls hadn't enjoyed much success earlier in his career. But as a

KEEP POUNDING

After he retired, Sam Mills became an assistant coach with the Panthers. In 2003, he learned that he had cancer. Mills gave a speech to the players. He said he planned to "keep pounding" in his battle with cancer. The Panthers made it all the way to the Super Bowl that season. Sadly, Mills died in 2005. But "Keep Pounding" turned into a powerful motto for the team.

Panther, he quickly became a star. He made the Pro Bowl in five of his seven seasons with the team. Walls still holds the Panthers record for receiving touchdowns by a tight end.

One of Carolina's greatest receivers was just a rookie in 1996. **Muhsin Muhammad** didn't get much playing time at first. But by the 2000s, he was one of the top receivers in the

NFL. In 2004, he led the league with 1,405 receiving yards and 16 touchdown catches.

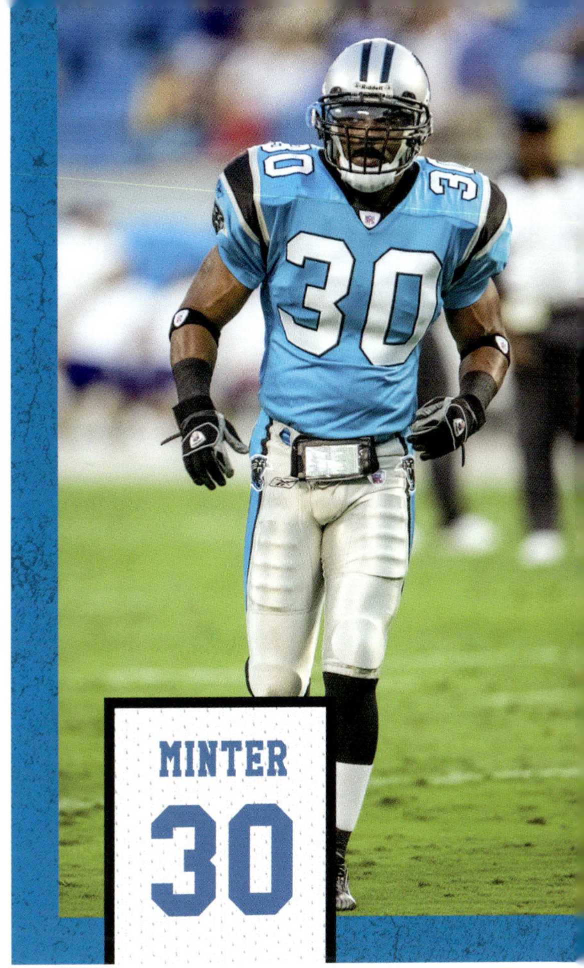

Safety **Mike Minter** joined the team as a rookie the following year. Minter went on to become a reliable defender for the next 10 seasons. During his career, he recorded 17 interceptions and made 805 tackles.

The Panthers struggled to build on the success of their 1996 season. But players like Minter, Muhammad, and Walls helped form a core for the future.

PEPPERS
90

CHAPTER 2
REACHING THE SUPER BOWL

The Panthers hit rock bottom in 2001. They had a record of just 1–15. But that gave them a high draft pick. They used it to select defensive end **Julius Peppers**. It turned out to be an excellent choice. In 2002, Peppers was named Defensive Rookie of the Year. In total, he spent 10 seasons in Carolina. Peppers was one of the best Panthers defenders ever. He was also one of the greatest pass rushers in NFL history.

Peppers instantly turned Carolina's defense into one of the league's best. At the other end of the defensive line was **Mike Rucker**. Opposing quarterbacks had nowhere to hide from this fearsome pair.

On offense, the Panthers had a top receiver in **Steve Smith**. Smith stood just 5-foot-9. But he was quick. And he ran his routes perfectly. Smith was always in the right spot for a catch. He ended up setting most of the team's receiving records.

Smith caught many of those passes from quarterback **Jake Delhomme**. Delhomme joined the Panthers in 2003. At the time, he hadn't started an NFL game in four years. But

STAT SPOTLIGHT

CAREER RECEIVING YARDS

PANTHERS TEAM RECORD

Steve Smith: 12,197

he proved to be a steady, reliable starter for the next seven seasons.

Offensive lineman **Jordan Gross** helped keep pass rushers out of Delhomme's face.

Gross played his entire 11-year career in Carolina. He started more games than any other Panther.

SUPER BOWL RECORD

In the fourth quarter of the Super Bowl, the Panthers had the ball on their own 15-yard line. On third down, Jake Delhomme tossed a bomb to Muhsin Muhammad. They connected on an 85-yard touchdown pass. The incredible play gave Carolina the lead with less than seven minutes to go. It was also the longest touchdown pass in Super Bowl history.

Everything came together for the Panthers in 2003. That season, the Panthers made it all the way to the Super Bowl. Delhomme threw three touchdown passes in the big game. Muhammad and Steve Smith each caught one. Carolina even held the lead in the fourth quarter. Unfortunately for Panthers fans, Carolina lost a heartbreaker to the New England Patriots.

GROSS
69

DAVIS
58

CHAPTER 3

RETURNING TO THE SUPER BOWL

The Panthers maintained a strong defense after their Super Bowl loss. Linebacker **Thomas Davis** joined the team in 2005. If opposing players got through the line, they rarely got past Davis. In fact, Davis made more tackles than any other Panther.

Defensive end **Charles Johnson** came to the Panthers in 2007. He didn't play much at first. But after Peppers left the team, Johnson took over as Carolina's top pass rusher. He ended up second behind Peppers on the team's list of most sacks.

In the 2010s, linebacker **Luke Kuechly** established himself as a monster in the middle of the field. But he also had great speed. That meant Kuechly could cover the entire field. He led the league in tackles twice. And he made the Pro Bowl in seven of his eight seasons.

On offense, Carolina had never had an elite quarterback. That changed when the Panthers drafted **Cam Newton** first overall in 2011. Newton exploded for more than 4,000 passing yards in his rookie year. But he was also a gifted runner. He recorded 706 rushing yards and scored 14 touchdowns that season. It was no

STAT SPOTLIGHT

CAREER PASSING TOUCHDOWNS

PANTHERS TEAM RECORD

Cam Newton: 182

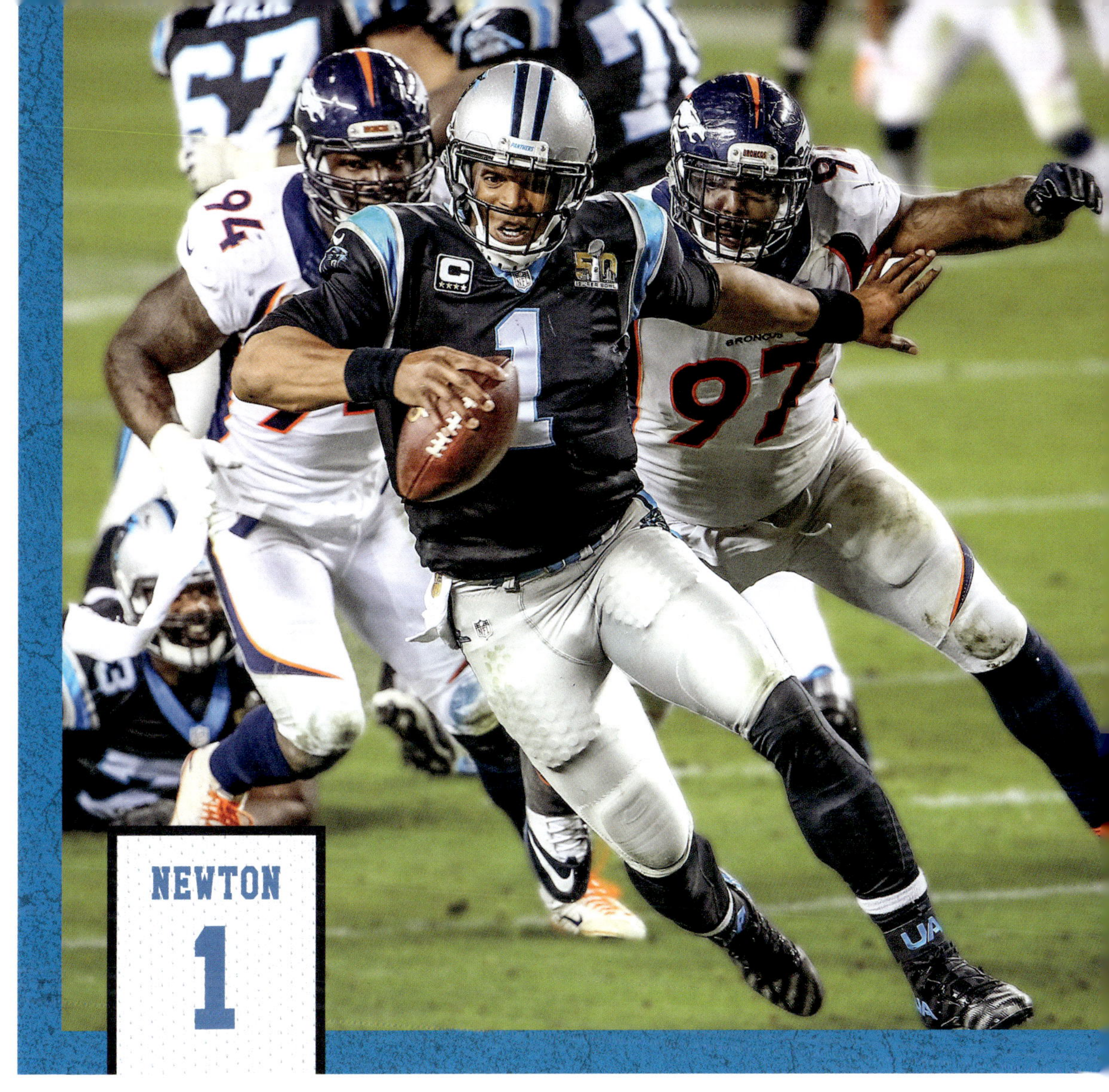

surprise when he was named Offensive Rookie of the Year.

Newton didn't do it all by himself. Offensive lineman **Ryan Kalil** provided great blocking.

Kalil made the Pro Bowl five times in his 12 years with the Panthers.

One of Newton's top targets was tight end **Greg Olsen**. Olsen was a fantastic blocker. He was also a great receiver. He recorded more than 1,000 receiving yards in three straight seasons. One of those seasons was 2015. That's when Carolina made a run to the Super Bowl. However, the game ended in heartbreak once again. The Denver Broncos beat them 24–10.

DOUBLE TROUBLE

Carolina had not one but two great running backs in 2009. **Jonathan Stewart** and **DeAngelo Williams** became the first Panthers teammates to each rush for more than 1,100 yards in a season. Stewart finished his career with the most rushing yards in Panthers history. Williams finished with the second-most.

Beginning in 2017, Panthers fans had a new star to cheer for. Running back **Christian**

McCaffrey was a talented rusher and great pass catcher. In 2019, he had the third-most yards from scrimmage in NFL history. Fans hoped he would be a part of the next Panthers Super Bowl run.

TIMELINE

1995
SAM MILLS
(1995–97)
KEVIN GREENE
(1996, 1998–99)
JOHN KASAY
(1995–2010)
MUHSIN MUHAMMAD
(1996–2004, 2008–09)
2000
WESLEY WALLS
(1996–2002)
MIKE RUCKER
(1999–2007)
STEVE SMITH
(2001–13)
MIKE MINTER
(1997–2006)
JAKE DELHOMME
(2003–09)
JULIUS PEPPERS
(2002–09, 2017–18)
JORDAN GROSS
(2003–13)
THOMAS DAVIS
(2005–18)
2010
RYAN KALIL
(2007–18)
CHARLES JOHNSON
(2007–17)
CAM NEWTON
(2011–19)
LUKE KUECHLY
(2012–19)
GREG OLSEN
(2011–19)
CHRISTIAN McCAFFREY
(2017–)
2020

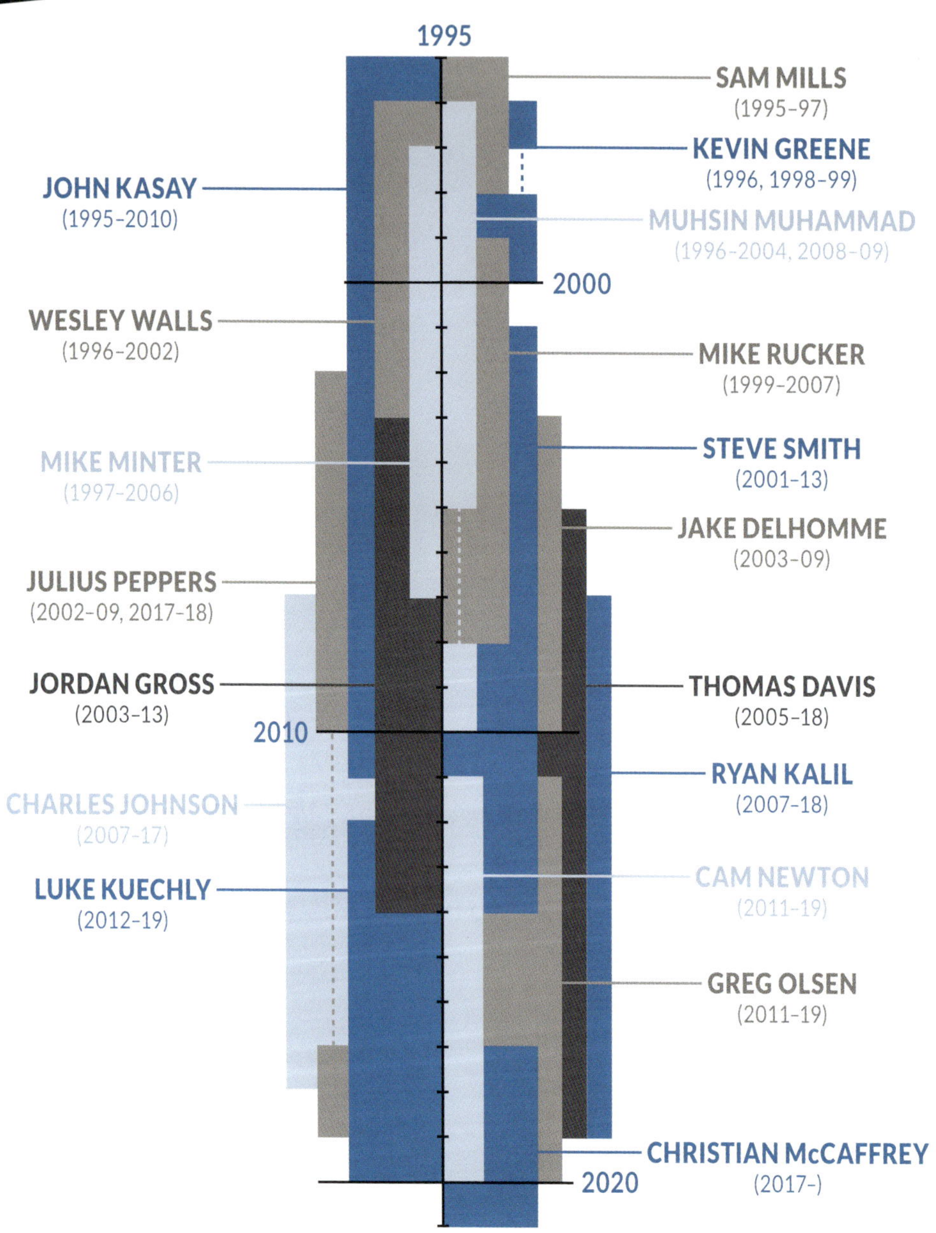

TEAM FACTS

CAROLINA PANTHERS

Founded: 1995

Super Bowl titles: 0*

Key coaches:

John Fox (2002–10), 73–71–0

Ron Rivera (2011–19), 76–63–1

MORE INFORMATION

To learn more about the Carolina Panthers, go to **pressboxbooks.com/AllAccess**.

These links are routinely monitored and updated to provide the most current information available.

*1966 through 2020

GLOSSARY

conference
A subset of teams within a sports league.

defensive end
A player who plays on either end of the defensive line and typically rushes the passer.

draft
An event that allows teams to choose new players coming into the league.

elite
One of the best.

linebacker
A player who lines up behind the defensive linemen and in front of the defensive backs.

rookie
A professional athlete in his or her first year of competition.

sack
A tackle of the quarterback behind the line of scrimmage.

veteran
A player who has spent several years in a league.

INDEX